Skills Builders

SB

YEAR 5

GRAMMAR AND PUNCTUATION

Sarah Turner

Acknowledgements

Every effort has been made to trace all copyright holders, but if any have been inadvertently overlooked, the Publishers will be pleased to make the necessary arrangements at the first opportunity.

Although every effort has been made to ensure that website addresses are correct at time of going to press, Rising Stars cannot be held responsible for the content of any website mentioned in this book. It is sometimes possible to find a relocated web page by typing in the address of the home page for a website in the URL window of your browser.

Hachette UK's policy is to use papers that are natural, renewable and recyclable products and made from wood grown in sustainable forests. The logging and manufacturing processes are expected to conform to the environmental regulations of the country of origin.

ISBN: 978-1-78339-725-9

Text, design and layout © 2016 Rising Stars UK Ltd

First published in 2016 by Rising Stars UK Ltd
Rising Stars UK Ltd, An Hachette UK Company
Carmelite House, 50 Victoria Embankment
London EC4Y 0DZ

www.risingstars-uk.com

All facts are correct at time of going to press.

Author: Sarah Turner
Educational Consultant: Madeleine Barnes
Publisher: Laura White
Illustrator: Emily Skinner
Logo design: Amparo Barrera, Kneath Associates Ltd
Design: Julie Martin
Typesetting: Newgen
Cover design: Amparo Barrera, Kneath Associates Ltd
Project Manager: Sarah Bishop, Out of House Publishing
Copy Editor: Hayley Fairhead
Proofreader: Jennie Clifford
Software development: Alex Morris

British Library Cataloguing-in-Publication Data
A CIP record for this book is available from the British Library.
Printed by Liberduplex S.L., Barcelona, Spain

Contents

GRAMMAR

PUNCTUATION

All of the answers can be found online. To get access, simply register or login at **www.risingstars-uk.com**.

1 Word classes

Different words do different jobs in a sentence. These are called word classes.

Word class	Definition	Examples
Nouns	tell you the names of people, places, feelings and things	Rohit, Adrian, Manchester, chair, love
Pronouns	replace a noun to avoid repetition	**He** played on **his** scooter. **That** is the best picture.
Adjectives	give you more information about a noun	the **big** dog a **blue** ball my **younger** sister
Verbs	tell you what is happening in a sentence	She **played** a game. They **are going** to the swimming baths.
Adverbs	explain when, why or how an action happens	I stroked the dog **gently**. She won the match **yesterday**.
Conjunctions	connect words, phrases and clauses	Ruby brushed her teeth **before** she went to bed. **If** it is raining tomorrow, we will need our umbrellas.
Prepositions	show the position of things	He put it **under** the chair. **After** supper we went to bed.
Determiners	always placed before a noun and help to define it	**All** children love to play games. **The** teacher read **a** book.

Activity 1

Using the table below, sort the following words into the correct categories.

car played silently he slowly Zeikel

Mina you school washed they

Nouns	Pronouns	Verbs	Adverbs

Activity 2

Label each of the words below as either a verb (V) or a noun (N).

a)

 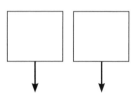

The lion approached silently as the zebra rested in the grass.

b)

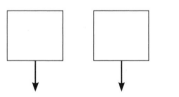

The baker kneaded the dough before leaving it to rise.

c)

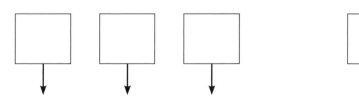

Yesterday we explored the beach and found some beautiful pebbles.

Activity 3

Circle the conjunctions in the sentences below.

a) Monique saw it all happen, yet she could not stop it.

b) The river has flooded because it has been raining a lot.

c) Although Adam likes music, he can't play any instruments.

d) You couldn't hear the music when the train went past.

e) My dog goes crazy whenever it sees a cat.

Activity 4

Choose the best determiners to complete the sentences below.

the   **a**   **an**   **this**   **most**   **other**   **all**   **that**

a) It was _____ enormous castle.

b) It had _____ lake and a tall tower with _____ most amazing views of the sea.

c) _____ doctors are committed to making patients better.

d) I don't want to go to _____ movie!

e) _____ children like to eat pizza.

Activity 5

Tick the preposition that would be best to complete both sentences.

a) The boy took a sandwich _____ his lunchbox.

The postcard was _____ my uncle.

with		beside		near		from	

b) You will find the library _____ the supermarket.

The girl hid _____ the chair.

before		behind		near		under	

c) The cat sat _____ the bush to shelter from the rain.

James walked _____ the scaffolding.

with		under		near		from	

Activity 6

Add a suitable adverb to each of the sentences below.

a) The branches of the trees swayed _____ in the strong wind.

b) Dave kicked the ball _____ into the net.

c) Halima was singing _____ in the shower.

d) Alina waited outside the head teacher's office _____.

e) The rugby team ran _____ into the changing rooms.

f) The passengers _____ fastened their seat belts.

Investigate!

Can you write a definition for each of the word types from this unit (noun, pronoun, adjective, verb, adverb, preposition, conjunction and determiner) and an example of how to use each of them?

2 Phrases and clauses

When learning about punctuation, it is helpful to understand the difference between a **phrase** and a **clause**.

Phrase	A group of words that may have nouns or verbs but does not have a subject 'doing' a verb.	some funny animals
Clause	A group of words that has a subject 'doing' a verb.	Some funny animals are running round the field.

There are different types of clauses that you are likely to have met so far.

Main clause	A complete sentence by itself.	Tia went swimming. Kim eats doughnuts.
Subordinate clause	Starts with a conjunction and does not make sense by itself.	because Orin likes singing

Activity 1

Identify whether the phrase or the clause has been underlined in the sentences below. Put a tick in the correct box.

	Phrase	Clause
The knight fought his way <u>through the forest</u>.		
The large batch of dough <u>took ages to rise</u>.		
<u>For four days</u> the child had a terrible hacking cough.		
<u>The doctor did a thorough examination of the patient and decided he would need to rest</u> for at least a week.		
<u>There are a huge number of people</u> living in the Borough of Barnet.		
Above the castle <u>lurked a menacing monster</u>.		
<u>All through the night</u> the rain fell.		
I'd like to go to Disneyland <u>for my dream holiday</u>.		

Activity 2

For each sentence, put a tick in the correct box to show whether the main clause or subordinate clause is underlined.

Sentence	Main clause	Subordinate clause
<u>I have violin lessons</u>, although I have not been playing for very long.		
<u>If you want to improve</u>, you must practise a lot.		
I practise every weekend, <u>even when it's the school holidays.</u>		
<u>Ben went swimming</u>, even though he was tired.		

Activity 3

Underline the subordinate clause in each sentence below. One has been done for you.

Lucy enjoyed playing football, <u>especially when Kofi asked her to take part</u>.

a) When she was standing next to her brother, Anita looked very tall.

b) Even though he had little patience, Robert enjoyed chess.

c) Although I like cycling, I would prefer to go swimming today.

d) While you go to the river, I will watch the football.

e) I like the winter because I can build a snowman.

Investigate!

Can you write three phrases, three main clauses and three subordinate clauses?

In your reading book, can you find a phrase, an independent clause and a subordinate clause?

3 Relative clauses

A **relative clause** adds extra information to the sentence.

The boy, **who speaks five languages,** went to school.

We use **that**, **who**, **what**, **where**, **which** or **why** to add the extra information. Two sentences can become one.

I bought a new bike. It was very shiny.

I bought a new bike **that** was very shiny.

Some relative clauses are non-essential. This means that they give us information that we don't necessarily need.

Lucas, **who served the soup,** didn't notice the banana skin on the floor.

Activity 1

Underline the relative clause in each sentence. One has been done for you.

Julie, <u>who lives in Australia</u>, is coming to visit this summer.

a) Any child who has forgotten their dinner money should go to the school office.

b) Ahmed is visiting Johannesburg, which is in South Africa.

c) I sent a letter that arrived two weeks later.

d) Rio, who found the necklace, handed it in.

e) The kite, which was broken, blew away.

Activity 2

Add a relative clause to these sentences, using **where**, **who**, **whose** or **which**.

a) My <u>teacher</u> told me to try my best.

b) The <u>boy</u> ran down the street.

c) I saw the <u>dog</u>.

d) "Don't cry," said the <u>girl</u>.

e) The <u>athlete</u> won the race.

f) She lived in a small <u>house</u>.

Activity 3

Complete the table to show whether each clause is essential or non-essential. Put a tick in the correct box for each sentence.

	Essential relative clause	Non-essential relative clause
His car, <u>which was very old</u>, broke down.		
People <u>who eat too much</u> tend to have poor health.		
The bike <u>that came last</u> had a flat tyre.		
The coat, <u>which was very old</u>, had holes in the sleeves.		

Activity 4

Circle the relative clauses in the sentences below.

a) My new kittens, who are called Spike and Spotty, sometimes climb up the wall.

b) Jamie won a trophy, which was a large gold cup, at his football competition.

c) My best friend, who lives in Wales, is great fun to play with.

d) The green car that was left outside the restaurant belongs to Martin.

Investigate!

Can you find four relative clauses from a book in the school library?

Looking through your reading book, can you find four sentences that have essential and non-essential clauses?

4 Adverbs of possibility

One of the ways we use adverbs is to show how possible or likely something is.

We might use **perhaps**, **surely**, **certainly**, **possibly**, **definitely** and **obviously**.

Adverbs of possibility usually come in front of the main verb.

Will they **definitely** be there?

We will **possibly** come to England next year.

However, they come after **am**, **is**, **are**, **was**, **were**.

They are **definitely** at home.

She was **obviously** very surprised.

Activity 1

Underline the adverb that shows possibility in each of the sentences below. One has been done for you.

<u>Perhaps</u> he is too tired to come to the party.

a) She was clearly very emotional.

b) I'm too busy tomorrow; could I possibly come the day after?

c) He has obviously misunderstood the instructions.

d) They are certainly going to be there!

e) Maybe the message was never received.

f) The sun will definitely rise in the morning.

g) I am possibly the last to arrive.

h) Kim is certainly the smallest girl I know.

Activity 2

Rewrite each sentence, putting the adverb of possibility in the correct place.

a) Dad will come home early today. (probably)

b) The car will become rusty with age. (inevitably)

c) I can't think of a better reason. (possibly)

d) The test won't be so hard next time. (maybe)

e) I will call if my plans change. (certainly)

f) I am going to make a complaint. (definitely)

g) We will be late if we don't leave now. (surely)

h) I am impressed by your efforts. (truly)

Activity 3

Look at the table below. Use each adverb of possibility in a sentence.

certainly	
definitely	
maybe	
possibly	
clearly	
obviously	
perhaps	
probably	

Investigate!

Can you write a sentence each about things that will certainly happen, probably happen and never happen? Then ask a friend to put them in order from very likely to very unlikely.

13

5 Modal verbs

Modal verbs are important for expressing a degree of certainty. The main modal verbs are **will**, **would**, **can**, **could**, **may**, **might**, **shall**, **should**, **must** and **ought**.

- I **will** have my dinner at school.
- I **might** go to the cinema later with my friends.
- You **should** wear a coat when it's cold.

Activity 1

Underline the modal verb in each of the sentences below.

a) I could help you if I had the time.

b) You should have told your teacher.

c) You must put your trousers on after your underwear.

d) I might go shopping after I have finished school.

e) Wasif will be an amazing scientist.

Activity 2

Choose the correct modal verb to complete each sentence.

a) Our school team _____ win the football match.

(would, ought, should)

b) We really _____ remember to take our swimming costumes to the beach.

(may, might, must)

c) Do you think it _____ rain today?

(might, can, ought)

Activity 3

Tick the correct modal verb to complete each sentence.

a) Megan _____ like to go to the party.

Tick **one** of the following.

shall		ought	
will		would	

b) I wish I _____ be an astronaut.

Tick **one** of the following.

can		could	
will		would	

c) You _____ listen to all the instructions.

Tick **one** of the following.

must		might	
ought		would	

Investigate!

How many modal verbs can you remember from memory? Write down as many as you can in one minute. Read a chapter of your reading book. How many modal verbs can you find?

6 Expanded noun phrases

We can add detail to a sentence by expanding the noun phrase. We do this by adding an **adjective**, **prepositional phrase** or **adverbial**.

Eva ate the **cake**. (noun)

Eva ate the **chocolate** cake. (adjective)

Eva ate the chocolate cake **in the café**. (prepositional phrase)

Yesterday, Eva ate the chocolate cake in the café. (adverbial)

Activity 1

Write an expanded noun phrase about each of these pictures.

a)

c)

b)

d)

Activity 2

Add an expanded noun phrase to complete these sentences.

a) Flora came out of school and ran towards _____.

b) Theo walked into the stable and collected the _____.

c) Areeshah enjoyed watching the _____.

d) Vanisha liked to eat _____.

Activity 3

Which of these sentences contain an expanded noun phrase?

Tick **two** boxes.

Sam considered how to climb the tree. ☐

Sam considered how to climb the tall, old tree. ☐

Sam carefully considered how to climb the tree. ☐

Sam considered whether to climb the tree. ☐

Activity 4

Underline the expanded noun phrase in these sentences.

a) I saw the shiny, new car near the house.

b) She was eating a hot, spicy soup.

c) The two angry cats chased each other down the street.

d) The spring flowers had some bright yellow petals.

e) I bought a warm green scarf for winter.

f) He was playing with the old, rusty, metal bike.

Investigate!

Can you find some expanded noun phrases in your reading book? Look for a sentence where an adjective, a prepositional phrase and/or an adverb have been added to describe the noun.

7 Relative pronouns

A **relative pronoun** links one part of a sentence to another. The second part of the sentence describes the first part.

The main relative pronouns are **who**, **whom**, **whose**, **which**, **that** and **what**.

Reuben is the person **who** plays the guitar.

Activity 1

Circle the relative pronoun in each of the sentences below.

a) So, this is the young boy who is so clever.

b) Shall we climb into the boat that is waiting for us?

c) The luggage that fell off the trolley was mine.

d) Those who do not understand must put up their hands.

e) She fell into the hole, which was in the middle of the garden.

f) Can you see the woman who is wearing a red hat?

Activity 2

Complete these sentences with **who**, **whose** or **that**.

a) The boy _____ won the race is called Simon.

b) This is the book _____ I left on the bus.

c) This is the man _____ rescued my daughter.

d) The letter _____ I wrote to the newspaper has been published.

e) The woman _____ keys we found gave us a reward.

f) The pen _____ you lent me is similar to the one I've lost.

Activity 3

Choose the correct relative pronoun to finish each sentence.

a) Their new house, **that/which** they bought quite cheaply, does need some fixing up.

b) The Flintstones, **who/whom** live next door to them, have volunteered to lend their tools.

c) Jessica, **that/who** works at the hospital, will still have to commute to work.

d) Zain, **whom/whose** company is nearby, will be able to walk to work.

e) That's Peter, the boy **who/whom** has just arrived at the airport.

f) The children, **who/which** shouted in the street, are not from our school.

Activity 4

Tick the box to show which type of pronoun has been used in each of the sentences.

	Personal pronoun	Possessive pronoun	Relative pronoun
Anil smiled. He had done it and <u>he</u> couldn't believe it.			
Jazeera owns the Frisbee. It is <u>hers</u>.			
I talked to the girl <u>whose</u> car had broken down in front of the shop.			
This is the girl <u>who</u> comes from Spain.			

Remember!

Personal pronouns:

I, you, he, she, it, we, they (used as the subject in a sentence)
me, you him, her, it, us, them (used as the object of a sentence)

Possessive pronouns:

mine, yours, his, hers, its, ours, theirs

8   Paragraphs

A paragraph needs to be built up carefully. In order to write a detailed paragraph in non-fiction, we can apply the **PEE** strategy.

- **P**: make a **p**oint
- **E**: **e**xplain the point
- **E**: **e**xpand or use **e**vidence

An example of this is given below.

P: It should be compulsory for children to wear school uniforms.

E: If all primary school pupils wear a school uniform, it will ensure all children feel part of the school community.

E: Also, it would save families money as school uniforms can be purchased cheaply from many supermarkets.

Activity 1

Using the PEE rule, number these sentences from 1 to 3 so that they are in the correct order to create a short paragraph.

a)
- I think this because mobiles, on average, cost less to run and you can do a lot more with them.
- Mobile phones are better than landlines.
- This evidence is supported by internet research. It suggests you are less restricted with mobile phones and can freely move without any wires.

b)
- Evidence shows that 93% of teenagers surveyed admired a famous person, proving that most celebrities are good role models.
- Celebrities are good role models.
- I think this because many teenagers look up to famous figures or celebrities.

Activity 2

Can you finish off this paragraph using the PEE structure? The first two points have been done for you.

P The lion is often considered to be the 'King of the jungle'.

E This may be because lions are at the top of the food chain and are feared by many other creatures.

E _____

_____

Activity 3

Choose your own theme and apply the PEE structure when writing your own paragraph. You could use the pictures below to inspire you.

P _____

_____

E _____

_____

E _____

_____

  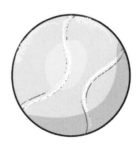

9 Linking paragraphs

All good writing is well organised. You should have a clear introduction, **paragraphs** that follow on from each other, and an ending.

A way to link paragraphs is to refer back to something in an earlier paragraph. You can use **pronouns** to do this.

Another way to link paragraphs is to show that periods of time have passed. You can use conjunctions to help you do this. Here are some examples.

To add more information	To offer a contrast	To explain a point	To sequence
In addition	But	Because	First
In the same way	However	As a result of this	Then
Furthermore	Although	Therefore	After that
Similarly	In contrast	Consequently	Finally

Activity 1

Look at the sentences below and change the bold words into pronouns.

a) Michael was late for school and **Michael** was going to get into trouble!

b) Sarah was going to Gran's house for tea and **Sarah** was very excited.

c) The kittens were very playful all morning and now **the kittens** were tired.

d) Gemma and I were swimming yesterday and **Gemma and I** swam fifty lengths together.

Activity 2

There are two pieces of writing below: one about deserts and the other about owls. The pieces of writing have been jumbled up. Read each of the extracts and decide whether it is an introduction (**I**), a main text (**M**) or a conclusion (**C**).

A desert has an inhospitable climate but people, animals and plants have all learned to adapt and make the most of its resources.

The barn owl is one of nature's most graceful hunters. Many organisations in Britain, such as the Barn Owl Trust in the South West, are working towards their conservation.

The barn owl is one of the most popular birds in Britain but is now extremely rare.

Only a quarter of deserts are made of sand. Some are covered in pebbles or bare rocks. In other areas, shallow lakes have formed after rain. Once these have dried in the sun, a flat layer of salt crystals is deposited.

When seen in flight, the general impression is of a large white bird. However, the upper parts are a beautiful golden buff colour, delicately marked in varying shades of buff and grey. It is only the face, breast and undersides that are mostly white.

A desert is a region that has less than 250 mm of rain a year. Rainfall often falls in violent downpours rather than evenly throughout the year.

10 Adverbials

An **adverbial** gives more information about a verb. Adverbials answer the questions **when**, **where**, **why**, **how** and **how often**.

The bus leaves **in five minutes**.

She promised to see him **last night**.

Fronted adverbials add more information about time and place. They can also be used to compare or conclude. Fronted adverbials are given at the beginning of a sentence and are followed by a comma. Some examples are given below.

Adverbs of time	Adverbs to compare	Adverbs to conclude
After a while,	On the other hand,	Generally,
Instantly,	Similarly,	In conclusion,
Immediately,	At the same time,	Actually,
Previously,		In fact,

Activity 1

Underline the fronted adverbials in these sentences. One has been done for you.

<u>During the night</u>, the horses escaped from the field.

a) Since it is too late, you will need to do your homework tomorrow.

b) While I was waiting for the tram, it began to rain.

c) In the south of England, there are many popular football teams.

d) If I have time, I will write to you.

Activity 2

Underline the adverbs and adverbial phrases in the passage below.

On Saturday, I woke up and went straight to tennis. My opponent played brilliantly, but I managed to win the match. Unfortunately, the café at the sports centre was closed, so we went home for hot chocolate. During the afternoon, I played in the garden with my sister. We built a den and hid quietly inside until teatime. That night, I ate dinner as if I hadn't eaten in days. I was worn out.

Activity 3

Add an adverbial phrase to each of the main clauses below to create a new sentence. Don't forget to add a comma. One has been done for you.

One sunny morning, Cameron walked through the forest.

Main clauses	Adverbial phrases
Cameron walked through the forest	In the dead of night
The police car came to a halt	One sunny morning
Divya stood underneath the lamp post	In the distance
There was a knock at the door	On the other side of the street
Catherine hurried to her car	All of a sudden
Jack lifted the curtain	In the depths of the countryside

Activity 4

For each sentence, write **five** new sentences, adding a different type of adverbial phrase each time. One has been done for you. Remember, adverbial phrases answer the questions **when**, **where**, **why**, **how** and **how often**.

The kite flew.

Yesterday, the kite flew. (when)

The kite flew **over the tall trees**. (where)

The kite flew **because I let go of the string**. (why)

The kite flew **faster than an aeroplane**. (how)

The kite **always** flew towards the trees. (how often)

a) The dog barked.

b) The baby cried.

c) Tomas walked down the road.

d) A lion roared across the savannah.

e) I drove my car.

Investigate!

How many adverbs can you name in two minutes?

Write some sentences containing adverbial phrases. Ask a friend to underline them.

11 Present perfect tense

Tenses are used to describe **when** something happened.

The **present perfect tense** of a verb describes an action that is completed over time or an action that begins in the past and continues in the present.

I **have** travelled.

She **has** travelled.

We use the **past participle** of the verb and add the verb **have** before it.

She **has lived** there for ten years.

Activity 1

Complete the following sentences using the present perfect tense. One has been done for you.

I <u>have</u> never <u>been</u> to Greece.

a) He _____ never _____ football.

b) _____ you _____ the magazine yet?

c) She _____ not _____ her lunch yet.

d) They _____ _____ the movie already.

e) We _____ _____ here for eight years.

Activity 2

Underline the present perfect tense verb phrase in each sentence. One has been done for you.

Megan <u>has sold</u> three cars this week.

a) The snowstorm is coming, but they have not closed the schools yet.

b) Samantha has felt uneasy about flying since she was a little girl.

c) Your team has developed a better mousetrap this time.

d) Olivia has arranged for your transportation to the island.

e) Ryan has solved more than half of the puzzles already.

Activity 3

Complete these sentences using the present perfect tense.

a) The children (found) _____ _____ the answers.

b) The team (played) _____ _____ in the Premier League for the last four years.

c) The children (eaten) _____ _____ cake and custard.

d) Grace and Alice (sing) _____ _____ in the choir.

e) I (slept) _____ _____ for over 12 hours!

Investigate!

Use some of the present perfect verb phrases to create a crossword with clues for your friends to complete.

How many examples can you find around the classroom that are written in the present perfect form?

12 Past perfect tense

Tenses are used to describe **when** something happened.

The **past perfect tense** of a verb describes an action that happened in the past, before something else happened.

I **had escaped**, before the guard noticed.

Before he went shopping, he **had been** cleaning his car.

Activity 1

Make sentences using the past perfect tense after the word **after**. One has been done for you.

Jan finished her dinner. Then she sat down to watch TV.

After Jan had finished her dinner, she sat down to watch TV.

a) George ate all the chocolate biscuits. Then he started eating the lemon ones.

_____

b) I turned off the lights. Then I went to bed.

_____

c) Lizzie did her homework. Then she went out to play.

_____

d) Our class got off the bus. Then we walked into the museum.

_____

e) Mei and Ana took the dog for a walk. Then they ate lunch.

_____

Activity 2

Fill in the missing words in the sentences below. Remember to use the word **had**.

a) I couldn't get in the house because I _____ _____ my keys.

b) The garden was wet because it _____ _____.

c) I knew I _____ _____ that man somewhere before.

d) The fridge was full of food because Mum _____ _____ the shopping.

e) Tom was in trouble because he _____ _____ some money.

f) Amy didn't play netball on Monday because she _____ _____ her arm at the weekend.

Activity 3

Complete the sentences below with the correct form of the verb in the **past perfect** or the **past simple** tense.

a) Unfortunately, when we arrived at Samantha's birthday party, all the guests _____ home so we did not meet anybody. (go)

b) I didn't take a map with me so obviously I _____ in London. (get lost)

c) I was really surprised when I heard that Steven _____ his exams. (fail)

d) Marvin returned to his home town after 15 years and he could not believe how much it _____. (change)

e) I did not get any reply to my email so I _____ to phone them. (decide)

Investigate!

Can you find a piece of writing from a reading book in the classroom that is written in the present perfect tense? Can you then change this to the past perfect tense?

13 Subject and verb agreement

A **singular subject** agrees with a **singular verb**.

The **box**   **is** small.

A **plural subject** agrees with a **plural verb**.

The **boxes**   **are** small.

Activity 1

Review each sentence and decide which verb should be added to the blank space. Use the present tense.

a) Ethan and Mariam _____ knocking on the door.

b) Logan _____ late for school.

c) Each man and woman _____ standing to attention.

d) The people _____ dressed in red.

e) The little boy, who was wearing jeans, _____ very stylish.

Activity 2

Review each sentence and look for errors in subject and verb agreement. If there is an error, write out the correct sentence.

a) She walk to the market.

b) The cat meows when he is hungry.

c) My favourite book are *Green Eggs and Ham*.

d) Ten minutes are enough time to get there.

e) The man and the woman were late for their appointment.

f) All of them is going to the parade.

Activity 3

Choose the correct form of the verb to agree with the subject in each sentence.

a) The dogs_____ barking. (was/were)

b) Jamie _____chocolate. (likes/like)

c) The boy _____toothache. (have/has)

d) Foxes_____ chickens. (eats/eat)

e) Who_____ it? (did/done)

Activity 4

Write these sentences correctly, ensuring that there is subject and verb agreement.

a) We was late for dinner. _____

b) She want a slice of birthday cake. _____

c) The bike have flat tyres. _____

d) Badgers lives underground. _____

e) She were swimming. _____

f) We was at school when the police car arrived. _____

g) The children always slides on the ice. _____

h) I wonder why you always shouts at me. _____

Investigate!

Have a look back through your own extended writing and check to see if there is subject and verb agreement.

Can you write the rules for subject and verb agreement for a friend to use?

14 I and me

I and **me** are personal pronouns that are used together when there is more than one person in a sentence. They are often used incorrectly.

To get it right, follow a simple rule: take the other person out of the sentence and see if it still makes sense.

The story was written by Tom and **I/me**.

To work out which we should use, take 'Tom' out of the sentence.

The story was written by **I**. ✗

The story was written by **me**. ✓

So the correct sentence is given below.

The story was written by Tom and **me**.

Activity 1

Put a tick in each row to show whether the word missing from each sentence is **I** or **me**. The first one has been done for you.

	I	me
Sarah and _____ both had a cold.	✓	
In the concert, Freddie and _____ sat next to Mr Tang.		
My mother drove Lin and _____ to the party.		
Nina, Kate and _____ are on the red sofa.		
Can you see _____ from over there?		

Activity 2

Choose either **I** or **me** to complete the sentences below.

a) James saw Chike and _____ up the tree.

b) Did you hear _____ call?

c) Adam and _____ finished before you.

d) When Jamila and _____ met, it was sunny.

e) Listen when Claire and _____ speak to you.

f) Come to the park with Sherrelle and _____.

g) Louis thinks you and _____ broke the window.

Activity 3

Write **Yes** if the sentence is correct or **No** if it's not.

	Is it correct?
Walk with I, me need the company.	
You and I should go to the market.	
Jake asked me to help him.	
If me go outside, I'll get cold.	
She and I have to going shopping tonight.	
Grace is going to watch me receive a prize.	✓

Activity 4

Cross out the words **I** and **me** when they are incorrect, and rewrite the words correctly.

a) You and I must tidy up the kitchen before Mum and me can start making the tea.

b) If you were to ask Jo and I, we wouldn't know how to answer.

c) Jack and me are better at working together than Noah and me.

d) Louis thinks you and me broke the window but Evie and I saw Alfie do it.

e) Nate and me need time to chat so can you and me go out later?

Investigate!

Can you write a set of rules to display around the classroom so that others know when to use **I** and **me**?

15 Using suffixes

You can use **suffixes** to change nouns and adjectives into verbs. Do this by adding **ate**, **ise**, **en** or **ify** to the ends of the words.

- author becomes author**ise**
- active becomes activ**ate**
- dark becomes dark**en**
- class becomes class**ify**

Activity 1

Add each of these words to the column with the correct suffix (to turn it into a verb). Some words may fit into more than one box.

advert   captive   pure   computer   fright   equal   personal   active
author   real   glory   hard   scandal   intense   light   liquid
hospital   false   sad   pressure   motive   terror   straight
note   central   material   legal

ate	ise	en	ify

Remember!

If the word ends in an **e** or a **y**, delete the last letter before adding the suffix.

glory ⟶ glor**ify**

pressure ⟶ pressur**ise**

Activity 2

Remove the suffix and write the root word correctly. One has been done for you.

standardise ⟶ standard

a) elasticate ⟶ _____

b) activate ⟶ _____

c) sharpen ⟶ _____

d) beautify ⟶ _____

e) loosen ⟶ _____

f) widen ⟶ _____

g) realise ⟶ _____

Activity 3

Add the correct suffix to each of the following words. Think carefully about the spelling rules. Some words may have more than one suffix. One has been done for you.

deep ⟶ deepen

a) less ⟶ _____

b) short ⟶ _____

c) improve ⟶ _____

d) length ⟶ _____

e) simple ⟶ _____

f) solid ⟶ _____

g) apology ⟶ _____

Investigate!

Can you write sentences using each of the new words you created in Activity 3?

16 Using verb prefixes

A **prefix** is a group of letters placed at the start of a word. The prefix changes the meaning of the word. Here are some common prefixes with their meanings.

dis	de	mis	over	re	pre
not	opposite	wrongly	too much	again	before
disconnect	**de**code	**mis**behave	**over**do	**re**apply	**pre**arrange

Activity 1

Choose the correct prefix to go at the beginning of these words. Can you find out what the new word means?

a) guide

b) confident

c) advantage

d) boot

e) school

f) agree

g) construct

h) spell

i) cycle

Activity 2

Match each of these prefixes to a word on the right to make a new word. One has been done for you.

dis   frost

de   coat

mis   appear

over   lead

re   paid

pre   born

Activity 3

Use the words below to complete these sentences.

dislike   **defrost**   **misbehave**   **overnight**   **rebuild**   **preview**

a) We had to wait for the freezer to _____.

b) The family stayed _____ at a hotel.

c) When the bridge collapsed, they had to _____ it.

d) Class 5 went to see a _____ of the latest movie.

e) We can't go out to play if we _____.

f) I _____ eating carrots.

Activity 4

Explain what these words mean now the root word has a prefix added to it.

a) mislead _____

b) overpaid _____

c) rewrite _____

d) decompose _____

e) disagree _____

f) prejudge _____

Investigate!

Can you write the rules for adding the prefixes **dis**, **de**, **mis**, **over**, **re** and **pre** for others to use?

Can you create a crossword for others to complete using some of the words you have created in the activities in this unit?

17 Using brackets

Brackets are sometimes called **parentheses**. Brackets show extra information. The sentence should make sense without the information in the brackets.

Last Monday **(the first day of school)** we went swimming.

Parentheses (or extra information) can be written between brackets, commas or dashes.

- Claire Taylor **(who lives in Bolton)** is an amazing singer.
- Claire Taylor, **who lives in Bolton**, is an amazing singer.
- Claire Taylor – **who lives in Bolton** – is an amazing singer.

Activity 1

Use brackets to punctuate the following sentences. One has been done for you.

I broke both bones **(the tibia and fibula)** in my leg.

a) My birthday 7th April is my favourite day of the year.

b) The school play which starts at 6 p.m. should be an amazing night.

c) The car which is a brand new Ferrari is shiny, fast and blue.

Activity 2

Tick **one** box below to show which sentence correctly uses brackets.

Cheetahs are (very fast) runners. ☐

The girl (who lives next door) plays the piano. ☐

I brush my teeth (in the morning) and at bedtime. ☐

When I stay up late (I feel really tired.) ☐

Activity 3

Add a pair of brackets to the following sentences.

a) Large owls can catch animals mice, rabbits, young foxes during the night.

b) Manchester a city famous for its football club is in the north west of England.

c) Every member especially any junior was encouraged to vote.

d) She was he thought a real nuisance.

e) In maths, we constructed or tried to construct regular hexagons.

f) He looked well, glared really at Theo.

g) Let's meet at the cinema the one behind the supermarket at 7 p.m.

Activity 4

Rewrite each sentence below, adding a pair of brackets in the most suitable place.

a) Mr Jones a governor at South Street Primary School will present the prizes.

_____

b) The elephant which comes from Africa can live for up to 70 years.

_____

c) The teacher who comes from Spain teaches at All Souls' Primary School.

_____

d) Miss Sally who loved chocolate was a dance teacher.

_____

Investigate!

Can you find examples around the classroom of punctuating extra information using brackets, dashes and commas?

18 Using commas

Commas help to signal meaning in writing. You must use a comma to:

- separate names, adjectives or items in a list

  Sarah invited Lindsey, Shelly, Kin and Donna to the wedding.

- separate extra information from the rest of the sentence

  Eva's teacher, Mrs Lewis, was really kind and helpful.

- separate subordinate clauses from a main clause.

  Even though they had cleaned the classroom,
  there was still a lot to do.

Activity 1

Rewrite each sentence, adding two commas for meaning to each one.

a) My teacher Miss Kinlock used to live in France.

_____

_____

b) The trumpet which is made of metal is a woodwind instrument.

_____

_____

c) The dog which is brown ran after the cat.

_____

_____

d) My best friend called Keira lives in Scotland.

_____

_____

Activity 2

Add commas to the sentences below to clarify meaning.

a) Running as fast as she could Kim raced her sister to the end of the road.

b) Michelle wearing a blue dress went out to the party.

c) Sophie a mother of two booked a holiday to Disney World in Florida.

d) On Monday at 9 a.m. we have an assembly.

e) The tree blowing wildly in the wind lost a branch.

f) Before I fell asleep I realised just how much I was dreading the next day.

Activity 3

Tick the sentences that use commas correctly.

Whenever, she went out, it was fantastic.	
Although he found the ball, he didn't tell anyone.	
Midnight, my black cat likes catching mice.	
Mrs Black, our head teacher, takes assemblies.	
Areesha and Waqas, my best friends, can run very fast.	

Investigate!

Can you write the three rules for using a comma to display around the classroom?

Can you write an example for each of the rules?

19 Using dashes

Dashes do the same job as brackets. They surround extra information in a sentence.

Mrs Moore – **who was new to the school** – was instantly loved by the children!

Single dashes can be used to emphasise a final comment or to add suspense.

Final comment	I'd love to go out with you for dinner – if you pay for it!
Suspense	As the window creaked open, I turned around and saw – a stranger.

Activity 1

Which of the sentences below uses dashes correctly?

a) Tick **one** of the following.

Olivia – my best friend – is coming round this evening. ☐

I love toast – in the morning – and evening. ☐

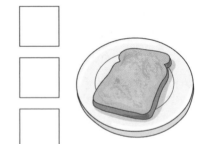

When I have a fizzy drink – it makes me giggle. ☐

b) Tick **one** of the following.

The cake was – lovely delicious in fact – so I had another slice. ☐

The cake was – lovely, delicious, in fact – so I had another slice. ☐

The cake was lovely – delicious, in fact – so I had another slice. ☐

Activity 2

Place a single dash in each sentence to make it correct. One has been done for you.

My mum said the man was very thoughtful – I don't know him.

a) "She got home, put the kettle on and sat down then she remembered."

b) As the cellar door scraped across the stone floor, I peered inside and saw nothing.

c) It was only when I squinted that I could see what lay at the bottom of the steps bones, lots of bones.

d) His writing was full of mistakes mistakes that could have been avoided.

e) The children cooled off in the swimming pool they had a lot of fun.

Remember!

A dash is not a hyphen, it's longer! A hyphen is most often used to join two words for meaning (bad-tempered).

Investigate!

Write some examples of how to use the single dash to emphasise a final comment or add suspense.